Exploring the Outdoors

Hiking

Gillian Richardson

MEDIA ENHANCED BOOKS
AV2
BY WEIGL™
ADDED VALUE • AUDIO VISUAL

www.av2books.com

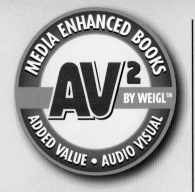

AV² provides enriched content that supplements and complements this book. Weigl's AV² books strive to create inspired learning and engage young minds in a total learning experience.

Your AV² Media Enhanced books come alive with...

Audio
Listen to sections of the book read aloud.

Key Words
Study vocabulary, and complete a matching word activity.

Video
Watch informative video clips.

Quizzes
Test your knowledge.

Embedded Weblinks
Gain additional information for research.

Slide Show
View images and captions, and prepare a presentation.

Try This!
Complete activities and hands-on experiments.

... and much, much more!

Go to **www.av2books.com**, and enter this book's unique code.

BOOK CODE

W 8 3 2 0 8

AV² by Weigl brings you media enhanced books that support active learning.

Published by AV² by Weigl
350 5ᵗʰ Avenue, 59ᵗʰ Floor
New York, NY 10118

Website: www.av2books.com   www.weigl.com

Library of Congress Cataloging-in-Publication Data
Richardson, Gillian.
Hiking / Gillian Richardson.
  p. cm. -- (Exploring the outdoors)
Includes index.
Summary: "Provides information about leisure activities that can be enjoyed in nature. Contains photos, charts, and healthy eating and exercise tips that encourage readers to get outdoors and enjoy hiking"--Provided by publisher.
ISBN 978-1-62127-355-4 (hardcover : alk. paper) -- ISBN 978-1-62127-361-5 (softcover : alk. paper)
1. Hiking--Juvenile literature. I. Title.
GV199.52.R53 2013
796.51--dc23
                    2012044675

Printed in the United States of America in North Mankato, Minnesota
1 2 3 4 5 6 7 8 9 0   17 16 15 14 13

012013
WEP301112

Project Coordinator: Alexis Roumanis
Art Director: Terry Paulhus

CONTENTS

All About Hiking

Trails and footpaths formed the first routes for people to travel from place to place. Once roads and railways were built, many people stopped walking along trails to travel. Most trails are now used for **recreational** uses, such as hiking.

People who like to walk may enjoy hiking. Many people hike to explore the outdoors and feel closer to nature. Hiking can offer an escape from city crowds. It is a way to find peace in a quiet country setting. Hiking is enjoyed by people of all ages and all parts of the world. People can go hiking throughout the year.

Many hikers visit Monument Valley, Arizona, each year to enjoy the rocky landscape and spectacular views.

Less experienced hikers can enjoy hiking on flat land and trails.

Hikers often develop an appreciation of nature. Some people hike to study and learn about rocks, trees, and wildflowers. They may watch or photograph birds and animals. Many hikers try to help protect the environment.

Building physical fitness is another reason people hike. Short hikes can be used as practice for longer, harder treks in the backcountry, or wilderness. Hiking offers a test of outdoor skills.

CHANGES THROUGHOUT THE YEARS				
PAST	People hiked as a means of travel.	People had to arrange their own hiking trips.	In winter, people wore snowshoes made of wood and leather to hike.	Hikers often used walking sticks made from tree branches to steady themselves on uneven ground.
PRESENT	People hike for fun and exercise.	People can arrange their own hiking trips or join a club that organizes group hikes.	People wear snowshoes made of metal and plastic.	Hikers sometimes use walking poles made of aluminum or wood.

Getting Started

Many people hike as a way to see places they cannot reach by car, airplane, or bicycle. Instead, they walk to these places. Often, hikers must climb over rocky ground or through forested areas. They may walk up steep slopes, through water, and downhill.

Very little equipment is needed for hiking. For a short or a long hike, wearing the right clothing and taking the least amount of gear necessary will make the trek more fun.

Sunglasses offer protection from the Sun's harmful rays.

All the Right Equipment

1 Wearing a hat while hiking has many benefits. A hat can protect hikers from the Sun or rain.

2 Sturdy, comfortable shoes are very important. A pair of running shoes work well. However, waterproof hiking boots give more protection to feet and ankles. Boots should have good grip for safe footing on rough or uneven ground. Hikers should choose light to medium weight boots. A hiker will tire more quickly wearing heavy boots.

3 A daypack is a backpack that is big enough to hold clothing, water, and food. There is room to include items, such as a map of the trail, a compass, and a first aid kit. A camel bag is a daypack that has a built-in water bag and drinking tube.

4 Most hikers wear two pairs of socks. This prevents the shoe from rubbing against the skin. Rubbing can cause blisters. Thin, nylon socks under a thicker wool or polyester pair are the best choice. These materials absorb moisture and keep it away from the skin.

5 Many hikers use walking or trekking poles. These poles can be lengthened or shortened to fit the hiker's height. The poles help balance the hiker. Poles also keep a hikers' arms moving. This exercises the arm muscles along with the leg muscles.

6 Hikers should dress in layers. In warm seasons, a T-shirt and shorts will work well during the day. A fleece or wool sweater should be packed in case the weather becomes cold. Windproof pants and a waterproof jacket are easy to carry for another layer of protection. Layers can be added or removed as needed.

Hiking Basics

Hiking can be done alone or with friends. Many people also enjoy hiking with organized groups, such as walking or **naturalist** clubs. One person sets a pace that is comfortable for all members of the group. Some hikers walk for about 30 minutes before resting for up to 5 minutes. Longer rest stops cause muscles to cool and stiffen. It is best to limit longer stops to meal breaks.

When choosing trails, consider skill level, the season, and the amount of time available for hiking. There are trails in city parks, national parks, and in the backcountry. Many trails are on public land, but some cross private property. Always ask permission to enter private land. Remember to leave gates as they were found, either opened or closed.

Proper hiking habits show respect for property, nature, and other hikers. It is important to stay on marked trails to avoid damaging the environment. Hikers should take care not to disturb wildlife or pick wild plants along the trail. Never throw garbage onto the trail. Hikers must take home any items they packed for their hike. This will allow the next hiker to enjoy the same natural experience.

To avoid blisters, it is important to keep your socks and shoes dry.

It is also important for hikers to think about the weather. Before setting out, check the forecast for the area and time of day. Take extra water along in hot weather to prevent **dehydration**.

Hiking in groups is safer than hiking alone. If one person is injured, someone from the group can leave to find help. Wildlife also tend to avoid groups of people.

Hiking Levels

The **terrain** and the length of the trip determine the difficulty of the hike. Level ground with a firm surface offers few problems for average hikers. Rocky, uneven ground or a narrow trail will make footing trickier. A gradual slope takes less energy to hike up or down than a steep trail.

Hikers can learn about a trail by studying a map, trail guide, or sign before setting off on their trek. They should practice on easy to moderate trails before taking on more difficult or challenging hikes.

Trails are rated easy, moderate, or difficult. An easy trail will be fairly short and have a mostly flat surface. Easy trails can be hiked by children and adults with little hiking experience and average fitness. Moderate trails are longer and may cover rough terrain. The most challenging hikes are rated difficult. They may cover steep **track** and rugged land. These challenging trails are for experienced hikers only.

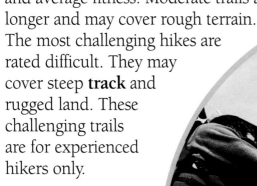

Hikers should use teamwork to avoid accidents and injuries on challenging hikes.

Hikers should carry a compass to show which direction they are traveling. A compass will always point north.

Rating systems vary around the world. In Chile, trails are marked by a color-coded signpost system that rates the difficulty of the trail. Some North American hiking guidebooks use shapes, such as circles, squares, and diamonds, in different colors. Hiking groups often post ratings for trails in their area on websites.

Hike Ratings

Easy ★
less than 2 miles (3 kilometers)
less than 250 feet (75 meters) change in elevation

Moderate ★★
2 to 4 miles (3 to 6 km)
Between 250 and 750 feet
(75 and 230 m) change in elevation

Difficult ★★★
more than 4 miles (6 km)
more than 750 feet (230 m)
change in elevation

Staying Safe

Well-maintained trails are the safest places to hike. However, hikers should still be cautious and watch for hazards. Careful planning and preparation can help prevent problems.

Hikers should always tell someone where they plan to hike, how long they will be gone, and when they expect to return. In the case of accident or injury, this information can help searchers track and locate a hiker more easily. Hikers should begin the hike early in the day. This will allow plenty of time to complete the route before nightfall. Hikers should also include time for regular rest stops along the way.

Resting helps hikers avoid injuries caused by fatigue, or tiredness. Resting also allows hikers to take time to view nature.

It is important to hike along well-marked areas and stay on the trail at all times. A map, compass, or **Global Positioning System** (GPS) will give directions, especially in an unfamiliar area. People hiking out of bounds or beyond marked trails will be more difficult to find if they become lost or injured. If hikers become lost, they should stay in one place. They can listen for others hiking nearby and yell, blow a whistle, or shine a flashlight to help searchers find them.

Hikers often see wildlife on a trail. Some animals, such as bears or cougars, can pose a danger. Pay attention to signs posted that warn the public about animals that have been spotted in the area. Watch for fresh tracks or **scat**. Talk or sing to warn bears that there are hikers on the trail. Never approach or try to feed a wild animal. Instead, back away and leave the area slowly, giving the animal plenty of room to move away.

Wildlife Tracks

Deer

Rabbit

Bear

Cougar

Wolverine

Explore the Outdoors

There are many other outdoor pursuits that involve hiking. Some of these are bird-watching, snowshoeing, geocaching, and scrambling.

Bird-Watching

Many people enjoy bird-watching while hiking. To bird-watch, hikers need binoculars and a bird guide or a list of birds found in the area. On a quiet walk, birds may fly by or perch on tree branches. Some birds can be identified by their calls. Bird-watchers can travel all over the world seeking rare species. A hike in the cloud forests of Costa Rica might reveal many exotic birds. People hiking in the Grand Canyon may see the endangered California condor.

Snowshoeing

Snowshoes are designed for walking on top of deep snow. They have a broad, flat, metal frame covered with plastic or nylon webbing. The shoes are strapped to the bottom of the hiker's feet. The broad surface spreads out a person's weight. This allows the person to walk on top of the snow. The first snowshoes were invented by North American Aboriginal Peoples. Their snowshoes had wooden frames and leather laces. The shoes helped them travel more easily in the deep snow.

Scrambling

Scrambling is a combination of hiking and climbing. Scramblers use both their hands and feet to hike over difficult and steep terrain. They do not use special gear. There are many trail guides that feature scrambling routes.

Geocaching

Geocaching is a game of hide and seek that involves hiking. A hiker uses GPS technology to find a location that another person has posted on a website. Here, the geocacher will find a small **cache**. Inside the cache is a log book and other items. The finder leaves a note, takes an object from the cache, and leaves another object for the next geocacher. Geocaching began in 2000 in Oregon. It has spread to many countries around the world.

Hiking Around the World

1 West Coast Trail, Canada
Created in 1907 to help rescuers reach shipwrecks, this 47-mile (76-km) trail hugs the southwestern coast of Vancouver Island, British Columbia. Easier sections follow sandy beaches, but the southern portion is a difficult hike.

2 The Appalachian Trail, United States
Stretching from Maine to Georgia, this 2,175-mile (3,500-km) trail winds through the Appalachian Mountains and offers every level of difficulty.

3 The Inca Trail to Machu Picchu, Peru
This trail climbs 28 miles (45 km) through mountainous jungle to its highest point at 13,780 feet (4,200 m). Views include cloud-forest, jungle, and Inca ruins.

4 Grindelwald, Switzerland
During summer, more than 31 miles (50 km) of trails make Grindelwald the hiking capital of the Bernese Alps. Gondola rides, caverns, and glaciers are among the attractions.

Arctic Ocean

North America

Atlantic Ocean

Pacific Ocean

South America

SCALE

0   600 miles

0   1,000 Kilometers

Southern Ocean

iking trails can be found all over the world. They include every level of difficulty and type of environment. They also cover different distances. Below is a sample of hiking trails found around the world.

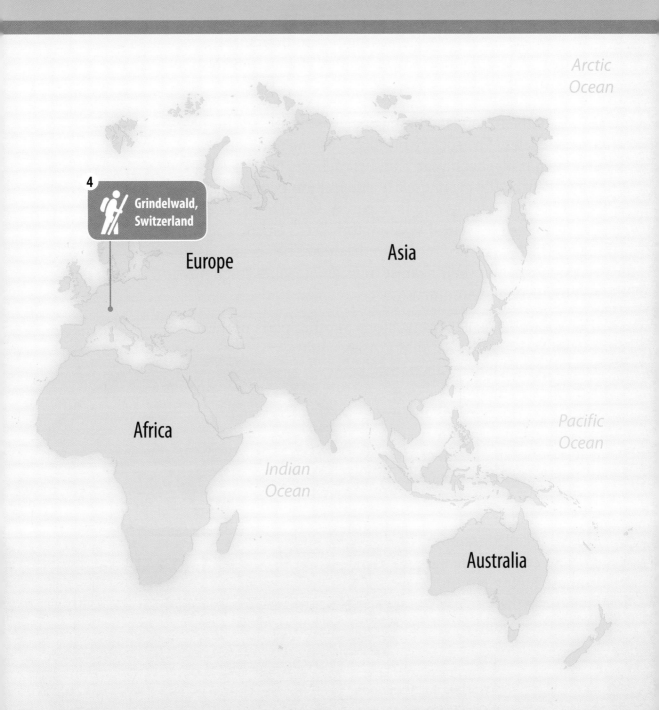

4 Grindelwald, Switzerland

Arctic Ocean

Europe

Asia

Africa

Indian Ocean

Pacific Ocean

Australia

Join the Club

There are many hiking clubs and organizations around the world. Most of them help members improve their physical fitness while enjoying the outdoors. Many hiking clubs do not host competitions. Hikers must test their own skill level.

In 1976, the American Hiking Society was formed in the United States. The society promotes hiking and helps maintain trails. Each year, the society hosts National Trail Days. During the event, nearly one million people visit trails to view exhibits and take part in workshops. Events are held in all 50 states, Washington, D.C., Guam, Canada, Puerto Rico, and the U.S. Virgin Islands. The society also helps hikers find their nearest trails and teaches them how to protect the environment.

There are clubs and organizations in other parts of the world. In 1936, the Ramblers' Association began in the United Kingdom. The Ramblers encourage walking and help improve walking conditions in the countryside of Great Britain. Members of the Federated Mountain Clubs of New Zealand go tramping together. Hiking is called tramping in New Zealand. All of these hiking groups encourage the safe use of the backcountry.

The American Hiking Society builds bridges over rivers and ravines.

For day-long hikes, hikers should pack sunscreen, a first aid kit, energy bars, and water.

Healthy Habits

People often find hiking more enjoyable and less tiring when they keep fit with regular exercise, such as walking, swimming, and biking. Hiking itself is a way to increase fitness. It builds strong leg muscles and helps keep lungs healthy and working well.

Exercise, such as stair climbing, improves breathing. Strong lungs are important to maintain a steady pace over long distances. Walking with a light backpack is important for hikers who will carry heavier items needed for comfort and safety on longer treks.

A well-balanced diet improves overall fitness. Healthy meals include fruits, vegetables, dairy, grains, and protein. Healthy snack foods to pack along on a hike may include granola bars, carrot sticks, and sandwiches. Another nutritious choice is trail mixtures of nuts, chocolate, and dried fruit. Hikers call these mixtures gorp. Gorp stands for "good old raisins and peanuts."

Proper nutrition is an important part of staying healthy. Fruits and vegetables are a source of energy and nutrition.

Hiking Tip #3

Hiking in the Sun can cause dehydration. Drinking plenty of water is the best way to stay hydrated.

While hiking, it is important to drink plenty of water. Each hiker should carry his or her own supply of water. Do not drink from lakes or streams, as the water may not be safe to drink. Some sources of water may carry **bacteria** that can cause illness.

Gorp Recipes

There are many different gorp recipes. Try making your own gorp mix, or use one of the following recipes.

GORP RECIPE 1
- 1/3 cup dates
- 1/3 cup M&M's
- 1/3 cup peanuts
- 1 cup coconut
- 1 cup low-fat granola

GORP RECIPE 2
- 1 cup almonds
- 1 cup peanuts
- 1 cup raisins
- 1 cup low-fat granola
- 1 cup dried apple

GORP RECIPE 3
- 1/3 cup peanuts
- 1/3 cup raisins
- 1/3 dried apricots
- 1 cup shelled sunflower seeds

GORP RECIPE 4
- 1 cup M&M's
- 1 cup almonds
- 1 cup raisins

Brain Teasers

Test your hiking knowledge by trying to answer these brain teasers.

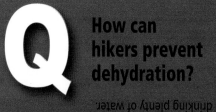

Q How can hikers prevent dehydration?

A: Hikers can prevent dehydration by bringing and drinking plenty of water.

Q Why should hikers not wear heavy boots?

A: Hikers should not wear heavy boots because the extra weight will cause hikers to tire more quickly.

Q Why is it a good idea to only take short rests when hiking?

A: Long rests allow muscles to cool and stiffen.

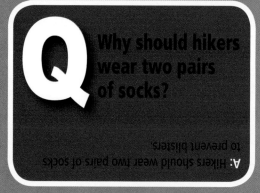

Q Why should hikers wear two pairs of socks?

A: Hikers should wear two pairs of socks to prevent blisters.

Q What special equipment do hikers need to watch birds?

A: Bird-watchers need binoculars and a bird field guide or list of birds found in the area.

Q What is gorp?

A: Gorp is a popular trail mix that may consist of nuts, dried fruit, and chocolate.

Key Words

bacteria: tiny, living cells that can cause illness

cache: waterproof container

dehydration: an abnormal decrease in body fluids

Global Positioning System (GPS): a system using satellite signals to find a location on Earth

naturalist: person who studies nature

recreational: something done for fun or relaxation, such as hobbies, games, and sports

scat: animal droppings

terrain: the ground

track: a rough path

Index

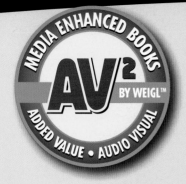

Log on to www.av2books.com

AV[2] by Weigl brings you media enhanced books that support active learning. Go to www.av2books.com, and enter the special code found on page 2 of this book. You will gain access to enriched and enhanced content that supplements and complements this book. Content includes video, audio, weblinks, quizzes, a slide show, and activities.

AV[2] Online Navigation

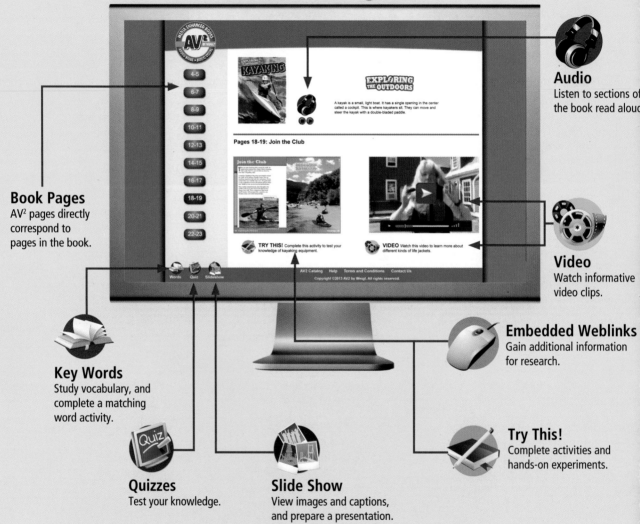

Book Pages
AV[2] pages directly correspond to pages in the book.

Audio
Listen to sections of the book read aloud

Video
Watch informative video clips.

Key Words
Study vocabulary, and complete a matching word activity.

Embedded Weblinks
Gain additional information for research.

Quizzes
Test your knowledge.

Slide Show
View images and captions, and prepare a presentation.

Try This!
Complete activities and hands-on experiments.

AV[2] was built to bridge the gap between print and digital. We encourage you to tell us what you like and what you want to see in the future.

Sign up to be an AV[2] Ambassador at www.av2books.com/ambassador.